Theo Adam
minister
Oak Hill Pres. Church.
Saint Louis
1955

WHAT IS CHRISTIAN CIVILIZATION?

WHAT IS
CHRISTIAN CIVILIZATION?

BY

JOHN BAILLIE, D.D., D.Litt., S.T.D.

Professor of Divinity in the University of Edinburgh

NEW YORK

CHARLES SCRIBNER'S SONS

1945

FOREWORD TO AMERICAN EDITION

These chapters were first delivered, in the spring of this year, as the Seventeenth Series of Riddle Memorial Lectures in the University of Durham; and as such they are being published in England. But they also formed the substance of the Hoyt Lectures which I delivered in July on the Auburn Seminary Foundation in Union Theological Seminary, New York City; and they were used as the basis of lectures addressed to conferences of ministers in Pittsburgh, Princeton and Chicago in June and July.

I should like to take this opportunity of thanking those responsible for these conferences for their kindness in wishing me to participate in them. It was a special honour and pleasure to be the Hoyt Lecturer, both because it meant a further association with the two seminaries, Auburn and Union, where I had spent so many happy years, and also because among all the colleagues of my early teaching days there was none whose friendship I valued more than that of the late Dr. Arthur S. Hoyt.

JOHN BAILLIE

August, 1945.

CONTENTS

I

THE HISTORICAL RELATIONS OF CHRISTIANITY AND CIVILIZATION

'THE Battle of Britain', said Mr. Churchill on the 18th of June 1940, 'is about to begin. Upon this battle depends the survival of Christian civilization.' It is this concept of Christian civilization that I should like to discuss. I desire to ask in what sense any possible civilization can be said to be Christian, how far either any past order of things or our present one merits such a description, and what the prospects are for the future. It is natural that I should begin with something of an historical reminder, though in offering it I shall have to lean heavily upon the conclusions reached and the impressions formed by scholars whose acquaintance at first hand with the primary documents is such as I can myself only very occasionally claim to possess.

The word 'Christian' was first applied, not to a civilization, but to certain individuals who formed an insignificant minority within the great civilization of the ancient Roman Empire. It was a name used by the citizens of Antioch to designate the followers of Christ about a dozen years after their Master's death. Though at first perhaps only a nickname, it came before very long to be used by the Christians themselves, and soon afterwards appears as part of their name for the spiritual community in which they felt themselves to be united—the Christian Church. There is therefore no doubt that a community as well as an individual may be rightly spoken of as Christian. Our question is only how the word may be applied to a civilization.

The difficulty of this question has no parallel in the history of earlier religions and civilizations, since in ancient societies there was nothing corresponding to the distinction, now so familiar to us, between Church and general community. Nor had there been anything corresponding to it in the early history of that ancient society which formed the background of the Christian movement, namely, ancient Israel. Here the nation had itself been a holy community in the very fullest sense, God's own chosen and peculiar people. With the nation God had made His covenant, and to the nation He had given His promises. 'The community of true religion and the political community of Israel' were never, according to Robertson Smith, 'separated even in thought.'[1] But with the appearance of the great prophets of the eighth century B.C. a new conception begins to emerge. The prophets were bitterly critical of the state into which the life of the nation had fallen. They regarded the chosen people as largely given over to apostasy, with only a few left who were faithful; but in the continued faithfulness of this remnant their hopes were centred. They believed such a remnant would always be there, that it alone was now the true Israel of God, and that to it the promises would still be fulfilled. Naturally the distinction thus drawn by the prophets was not always welcome to the priests, but it was a necessary preparation for early Christian history, which continues the prophetic tradition. The followers of Christ, finding themselves after their Lord's death to be a small and scattered minority within the vast and alien life of a pagan empire, were saved from the intolerable individualism of such a situation by their steadfast faith in another community within the imperial community and continuous with the faithful remnant of the ancient Israelite theocracy; while at the same time the dissociation of this community alike from Hebrew nationality and from Roman civilization enabled them to conceive of it as capable of extension among the people of every race and tongue and tribe under heaven.

The life of the early Christians within the Roman Empire thus introduces us to a sociological situation of a hitherto unfamiliar kind. How were they to relate the life of their own community to that of the general community within which they had to live? This question, according to Sir Ernest Barker, is 'perhaps the profoundest in history'.[2] It was not merely a question of the relations of sacred and secular such as might already have arisen within the Hebrew theocracy or such as would afterwards emerge in a Europe that had officially adopted Christianity as its faith. We think of sacred and secular as

---

[1] *The Prophets of Israel*, p. 275.

[2] In *Church and Community* (Oxford Conference Series), p. 45. See also Sir Ernest Barker's *Church, State and Study*, p. 133.

having to do with distinguishable aspects or spheres of the life of a single integrated community. But the Roman Empire had sacred things of its own, while on the other hand the first Christians desired their own common life to extend to much more than common worship; *habebant omnia communia*—'all they that believed were together, and had all things in common'.[1] Thus the problem was rather how a small community professing the true religion could exist within another and larger community professing a false one. *This* was the problem which the ancient Israelite exiles had failed to solve when in despair they hanged their harps upon the Euphrates willows and said, 'How shall we sing the Lord's song in a strange land?'

The solution reached by the Christians lay in the frank recognition of two complementary facts which were held in balance one against the other; first, that Roman civilization was essentially pagan; and second, that it nevertheless represented a certain high standard of equitable and orderly and law-abiding society. This most just conclusion was elaborated somewhat as follows. Like all other civilizations which took their origin from the legendary Tower of Babel, the Roman is a fallen civilization and belongs to the devil. Nevertheless God has His restraining hand upon it. When the present world-order comes to an end, the devil will indeed have his whole will with it, but meanwhile God is graciously concerned to restrict the more unruly results of its sinfulness, if only in order that the Church may meanwhile be able to survive and carry on its mission—or, as we might put it, in order to make the world safe for Christianity; and those who are now responsible for the government of the empire hold, as it were, His commission to administer the laws and execute justice. It is therefore God's will that Christians should submit themselves to the Roman rule. Like others they must pay the taxes, according to Christ's own injunction, 'Render to Caesar the things that are Caesar's, and to God the things that are God's.'[2] They must also obey the magistrates: 'You must be obedient,' writes St. Paul, '. . . for the same reason as you pay taxes—since magistrates are God's officers, bent upon the maintenance of order and authority.'[3] And St. Paul also states the matter in general terms:

[1] Acts ii. 44, Vulgate and A.V.; cf. also Acts iv. 32.
[2] Mark xii. 17; Matt. xxii. 21.　　[3] Rom. xiii. 5–6. Moffatt's translation.

'Every subject must obey the government authorities, for no authority exists apart from God; the existing authorities have been constituted by God. Hence anyone who resists authority is opposing the divine order. . . .'[1] There were, however, some laws on the statute-book which, if they should be invoked against them, the Christians could not possibly obey, namely, the laws concerning religious observance. Up to the time when St. Paul wrote the words just quoted these laws had not been invoked against the Christian Church, partly because the latter was regarded by the magistrates as no more than a sect of Judaism which, as an indigenous provincial cult, was accorded the privilege of a *religio licita*. Up to that time, indeed, St. Paul's experience of Roman rule had been mainly as shielding him from the designs of the Jews themselves. But when, some five years later, he himself appealed to Caesar, things were to turn out differently. The era of persecution now commenced, and from now onwards the Christians were constrained to distinguish the area of their rightful obedience from that of their necessary disobedience. They had to balance St. Paul's pronouncement that 'every subject must obey the government authorities' against St. Peter's words (spoken before the Jewish supreme court) that 'we ought to obey God rather than men'.[2]

Such then in brief was the attitude of the early Church towards the only civilization which it knew. It combined a necessary and not disloyal participation with a very large measure of spiritual detachment. The only society in which Christians would really be at home was the Kingdom of God, whose life they already enjoyed by way of foretaste, and for whose speedy consummation they eagerly hoped. '*Our* citizenship (πολίτευμα)', St. Paul had said, 'is in heaven, whence also we look for the Saviour, the Lord Jesus Christ, who shall transform the body of our humiliation into the likeness of the body of his glory by the power which enables him to subdue all things to himself.'[3] There are well-known words of St. Augustine which, though written much later and under the changed conditions of an officially Christian empire, express

---

[1] Rom. xiii. 1–2. Moffatt's translation.   [2] Acts v. 29.
[3] Phil. iii. 20. The word *our* is emphasized by its position in the Greek sentence.

very well the attitude of the citizens of this heavenly city towards the earthly city or civilization whose advantages they mean-while share with their pagan neighbours.

'There is a common use among both kinds of men and households', he writes, 'of the things necessary to this mortal life, but each uses them to its own peculiar and widely different end. For the earthly city, which does not live by faith, seeks an earthly peace; and interests itself in the harmony of rule and obedience among its citizens to the end that there may be a certain agreement of men's wills regarding the things that pertain to this life. But the heavenly city, or rather that part of it which only makes pilgrimage in mortality and lives by faith, is likewise obliged to make use of this peace, until that mortality which requires it shall pass away. Hence while it continues to live in the earthly city as a captive in its pilgrimage, though having already received the promise of redemption and the gift of the spirit in pledge of it, it does not hesitate to conform to the laws of the earthly city whereby are administered the things suited to the maintenance of mortal life; and since this mortality is common to all, a harmony is preserved between the two cities in respect of the things which pertain to it.'[1]

The restless missionary activity of St. Paul and the un-diminished zeal of his followers are sufficient proof of the Christian hope that an ever-increasing number of the citizens of the earthly city would embrace the Christian faith and join with them in the fellowship of the Church. Yet there is at first little evidence of a hope that the Church would ever grow beyond the dimensions of a comparatively small minority. Nor is there any sign that the Christians looked forward to any such reform in the ways of general society as would be likely to work a substantial change in their attitude towards it. They would continue to the end, they thought, to be a people apart, with separate habits of life, absenting themselves from the gladia-torial games and other spectacles, and having troubled con-sciences about such things as their relation to commerce and military service. The modern inquirer will sometimes ask why, besides concerning themselves with the internal life of their own holy community, with the gradual enlargement of that community, and with setting the world a new standard of private charity towards the under-privileged, they did not also give their minds to the structural reform of society as a whole.

[1] *De civitate dei*, xix. 17.

There were, however, several good reasons why such a thought could hardly have occurred to them. Foremost among these was the fact that they had no voice whatever in the general affairs of the empire and were far from imagining that they ever would have such a voice. There was further their strong persuasion that the days of earthly civilization were all but numbered, the consummation of Christ's Kingdom being very near at hand. Moreover, quite aside from any computation of the length of the interim period, it was on the coming of that Kingdom that their own hopes were set, rather than on the future prospects of any earthly order. No less than the enthusiasts of modern times they had their own Utopia, their own perfectionism, their minds being continually filled with the expectation of a Golden Age; but they were precluded by the very essence of the Christian teaching from believing that this perfection and this ideal quality of life were attainable by human effort within a fallen world. The modern inquirer will sometimes reply, 'No doubt they were so far right; and no doubt there is here a true insight which rebukes the dangerous illusionism and utopianism of so many modern revolutionaries; but can there not be at least some further approximation on the part of our earthly society to the life of Christ's perfect Kingdom?' To this, however, the early Christians would have answered in their turn that such an approximation is indeed to be hoped for, but only by the extension of Christ's influence over men's wills, and therefore by the expansion of the Church, and not by any change in the legislative structure of the civil order; if only for this reason, that the organizing principle of Christ's Kingdom is love, whereas the organizing principle of the civil order is compulsion backed, where necessary, by force.

The great and unforeseen change which was soon to overtake the situation was due to the remarkable success of the Christian mission. By the end of the third century the Church, though still suffering bitter persecution, was represented by a large and influential minority in almost every part of the empire, as well as beyond its borders. Historians are chary about estimating the size of this minority, and such estimates as they do give differ very widely. Gibbon thought that it amounted to only one-twentieth of the whole population; later estimates vary

from one-tenth to one-fifth.[1] However that may be, the fourth
century opened a new chapter. The ninth and tenth generations
of Christians were to see 'the powers that be' themselves embrace the Christian faith, the emperor and his court becoming
members of the Church. In the ancient world the effects of
such an event could not fail to be dramatic, for a community's
religion was in those days so integral a part of its general life
that the conversion of the rulers must almost inevitably mean
the conversion of the community as a whole. It was taken for
granted that a state must have some 'established religion', and
when the laws establishing the old religion of Rome were now
abrogated, other laws establishing the Christian religion had to
be put in their place. It would be a long time before the old
rites would altogether cease to be observed, but it would be
mainly in the country districts that these observances would
continue, and that is why those who still observed them came
to be spoken of as *pagani*, which means only countryfolk. It
was now the turn of the pagans to be persecuted; and, after a
brief experiment in toleration under Constantine, there followed
the destruction of pagan shrines and the martyrdom of some
pagan worshippers. However, the persecution of pagans by
the Christian emperors never approached the severity and bru-
tality of the persecution of Christians by the pagan emperors,
and there was as yet no general compulsion to observe the new
rites but at most a prohibition of the old. Moreover, it was
inevitable that the majority of Romans would themselves desire
to follow their emperor in embracing the new faith; and when
in the year 388 Theodosius put to a full meeting of the Roman
Senate the question whether the worship of Jupiter or the worship of Christ should henceforth be the religion of the Romans,
the latter alternative was carried by a large majority, and immediately the great and newly erected Lateran and Vatican basilicas
found themselves unable to cope with the crowds seeking baptism. And where Rome led, the rest of the empire would be
likely to follow. 'Rome', says Gibbon, 'submitted to the Gospel;
and the vanquished provinces had not yet lost their reverence
for the name and authority of Rome.'[2] But indeed Theodosius

[1] See Harnack, *The Expansion of Christianity in the First Three Centuries*,
English translation, vol. ii, pp. 452 ff.; Latourette, *History of the Expansion of
Christianity*, vol. i, p. 108.　　　　[2] *Decline and Fall*, ch. xxviii.

had eight years previously, and immediately after his own baptism, issued the edict *Cunctos populos* which began with the words, 'It is our desire and will (*volumus*) that all the peoples which are governed by the moderation of our clemency should follow the religion which was given to the Romans by St. Peter the Apostle. . . .'[1]

The end of the ancient Roman Empire was now close at hand, but this was on the whole so far from adversely affecting the expansion of the Church that during the following Dark Ages its membership came to include virtually the whole population of Italy and of many of the outlying dominions into which the empire was now broken up; nor yet was its relation to the civil authorities seriously affected, since most of the barbarian rulers themselves embraced the new faith. Indeed, we may say that during the following three hundred years, when the West had no emperor and no imperial administration, Christianity became the main agent of the continuity of its history and of such unity of cultural tradition as it still possessed. Even Mr. H. G. Wells gives to the section of his *Outline of History* which covers this period the heading 'The Salvation of Learning by Christianity'.

It is therefore the less surprising that when, at the beginning of the ninth century, the empire was reconstituted under a Frankish king, Christianity was now to be regarded as the very principle of its integration. Charlemagne's vision was of a universal civilization whose unity should be that of 'one Lord, one faith, one baptism', though it would still have one rule in things temporal and another in things spiritual. It is perhaps here, if anywhere, that we have the first clear concept of a Christian civilization. True, the vision seemed soon enough to fade and to be followed by a period of almost chaotic confusion; but within three centuries it was revived under the influence of the powerful personality of Hildebrand. And now a final step was taken, whereby the temporal rule was definitely subjected to the spiritual, i.e. the emperor to the pope. Henceforward, and throughout the Middle Ages, Church and empire will no longer designate two societies, but only two organs of a single society conceived as definitely and universally Christian.

[1] *Codex Theodosianus*, XVI. i. 2: *vide* Carl Mirbt, *Quellen zur Geschichte des Papsttums*, 3te Auflage, p. 45.

The whole of society is a *corpus Christianum*, and every depart-
ment of its life is under control of the Church which is, in its
more specific character, *corpus Christi*.[1] Christianity is therefore
now compulsory. *Quicunque vult* finally gives place to *compelle
intrare*, as it had long been foreshadowed that it would. Every
member of society is obliged to make Christian profession; all
children are baptized in infancy into the membership of the
Church; and exclusion from the sacraments carries with it the
loss of civil rights, the only concessions allowed being to certain
foreign ingredients in the population, the wandering Jew and
in some places the colonizing Mussulman. As Sir Ernest
Barker says, 'The excommunicated person could not enter
either the Church or the law court; could not receive either the
eucharist or a legacy; could not own either a cure of souls or
an acre of soil.'[2] Or as Dr. Figgis puts it, 'The word Churchman means to-day one who belongs to the Church as against
others. In the Middle Ages there were no others, or if there
were, they were occupied in being burnt.'[3]

This whole development from the Apostolic Age onwards
can be studied in all its parts and in great detail in Dr. Kenneth
Latourette's encyclopaedic *History of the Expansion of Christianity*, and I may be allowed to quote the following summary
of it from the same pen. From the time of Constantine and
Theodosius onwards, he writes, 'conversion was by the community as a whole rather than by individuals. To be sure, mass
baptism was practically always preceded by the baptism of a
few scattered families. Eventually, however, the community
as a whole adopted Christianity. Sometimes this step was taken
because of the example set by the leaders. In other instances
the leaders coerced the subject majority into following them to
the baptismal font.'[4] 'It was thus that Christianity had been

[1] 'In the Middle Ages Church and State in the sense of two competing
societies did not exist. . . . Nobody in the Middle Ages denied that the king was
God's minister, or that the bishops were great lords in the commonwealth. Pope
and emperor, when they quarrelled, quarrelled like brothers, as members of the
same society, the *civitas Dei*.'—J. N. Figgis, *Churches in the Modern State*,
pp. 190, 199.
[2] *Church, State and Study*, p. 66.
[3] *Churches in the Modern State*, p. 189. Dr. Figgis goes on to say that in the
Middle Ages a Churchman meant what we now mean by an 'ecclesiastic'.
[4] In *Church and Community* (Oxford Conference Series), p. 6.

adopted by the Roman empire. It was by this process that it became the faith of Western and Northern Europe.'[1]

The Protestant Reformation of the sixteenth century signalized in many ways the collapse of the Medieval system, but it did not at first work any essential change in those aspects of it with which we are here immediately concerned. The ecclesiastical jurisdiction of Rome was now successfully challenged, but since this challenge was closely associated with the equally successful challenge to the civil authority of the empire on the part of the northern nations, it was not at first understood as carrying with it any relaxation of the former intimate connexion between Church and community. 'The foundation of Lutheranism', says Troeltsch, 'is the conception of an ecclesiastical civilization under the compulsory domination of religious ideas';[2] and no less is true of original Calvinism. Both systems continued to demand that all children be baptized in infancy, so that the whole population was included in the Church's membership. Both systems made the observance of divine ordinances compulsory, and absence a punishable offence. There is no room either in Luther's or in Calvin's idea of a Christian society for the recalcitrant unbeliever or even for the heretic. The best that they could suggest for either was emigration to a non-Christian (or heretical) country; and when the Reformation failed of a complete victory in the German lands, it was in this direction that a solution of the resulting problem was reluctantly looked for. By the Peace of Augsburg some of the German principalities were recognized as Roman and others as Lutheran, and Romans living in a Protestant principality, or vice versa, had to choose between conversion and removal; *cuius regio eius religio*.

None the less a change was at hand. Though the early Reformers did not themselves surrender the idea of a Church coextensive with the community, and of a community that should be compulsorily Christian in profession, the freedom

---

[1] *History of the Expansion of Christianity*, vol. iii, p. 51.

[2] *Die Soziallehren der christlichen Kirchen und Gruppen*, p. 513. There is a serviceable English translation of this great work by Miss Olive Wyon—*The Social Teaching of the Christian Churches*. Recent Lutheran historians have pointed out certain serious defects and omissions in Troeltsch's account of the Lutheran system, but these are not such as to affect the generalizations which I quote from him in this lecture.

which they had won for themselves over against Rome was to lead the way for other freedoms. The history of the two succeeding centuries is a history of the growth of tolerance. Compulsory Christianity finally came to an end. The heretic and the professed unbeliever were soon allowed to exist in all states, and though they might still be excluded from many privileges, they were no longer denied ordinary civil rights. It is, however, equally important to recognize that the disappearance of compulsion did not of itself work any rapid change in the Church's hold upon the community, which still continued on the basis of general consent and long-established custom. It still remained true that membership of any national community almost automatically involved baptismal membership in one branch or other of the Christian Church. Thus a new type of Christian civilization here makes its appearance upon the page of history —what I shall call an open as contrasted with a compulsive Christian civilization. And not until towards the close of the eighteenth century did this situation begin to be overtaken by radical change. As Dr. Latourette reminds us, 'Even Voltaire was baptized and buried in consecrated ground'.[1]

§

As we now look back over the whole story, we see that the Christian Church, which had begun by thinking of itself as a faithful remnant continuous with the faithful remnant of the ancient Israelite theocracy, soon found itself beginning to be involved in a new theocracy of its own. A Church that had previously striven to have as little as possible to do with surrounding society was faced with an entirely new problem when the rulers of that society themselves became Christians; they had now to answer the new question, What should a Christian do when he is also a ruler?[2] How disturbing the question could

---

[1] *Church and Community*, p. 8.

[2] 'It is very interesting to compare Cicero's book *De Officiis* with the precepts of the Gospel. Infinitely less sublime and moving, it also differs from the Gospels in being concerned with a whole range of duties, administrative, judicial and military, which are outside the experience or imagination of the Asiatic villager or artisan. . . . One sees in every phrase the man of culture, the man with a stake in the country, the soldier, statesman, and governor. Such men were not to be found in the class from which the Christian movement arose.'—Gilbert Murray in *The History of Christianity in the Light of Modern Knowledge*, p. 48 f.

be becomes evident when we find Tertullian writing as late as the beginning of the third century: 'I own no duty to forum, battle-field or senate-house; I stay awake for no official employment; I take possession of no platform; I take notice of no councils; I avoid the voting-booths; I wear out no magistrate's bench; I trouble no courts of justice; I perform no military service; I govern nobody; I have seceded from the populace.'[1] Yet it was not merely the civil responsibility now perforce resting upon certain members of the Church that gave rise to the changed situation, but also the enormous increase of Church membership even in advance of the conversion of the rulers. This was bound to carry with it a lowering of the average standard of Christian commitment. Even in the earliest days the standard had of course not been uniform. From the beginning the Church had been in the habit of baptizing whole households, including the children and the slaves, at a single ceremony. Profession of belief and evidence of heart-felt conversion was demanded of each according to his capacity, but obviously nothing of this sort could be demanded of the very young, and no doubt less in the way of an autonomous decision was expected from the slaves than from their more intelligent masters. Meanwhile it was hoped that the Christian family would prove a school in which the younger and more backward members would gradually grow into the fullness of the faith. With the tenfold increase in the number of family groups desiring baptism which the next few generations were to witness, this variation in the degree of initial understanding and commitment was bound to become more marked. So long as the days of persecution lasted, there was on the whole little to encourage a half-hearted adherence, but it was different when the rulers themselves were converted and Christianity became the official cult of the community. There was now room for the greatest possible admixture of motives, and there were undoubtedly large numbers whose adherence was at first quite nominal. Writing at the beginning of the fifth century, St.

---

[1] *De Pallio*, 5. My colleague, Professor J. H. S. Burleigh, has drawn my attention to an even more apposite passage in Tertullian's *Apology* (ch. 21), which was written in 197 B.C. before its author became a Montanist: 'But even the Caesars would have believed on Christ, if either Caesars had not been necessary to the present world order (*saeculum*) or Christians could possibly have been Caesars.'

Augustine takes it for granted that 'those now fill the churches whom the winnowing [of God's final judgement] will separate out as on a threshing-floor'; so that 'many reprobate are mingled with the good, both being as it were gathered in together by the evangelical drag-net'.[1] Yet it was still held right that as many as possible should be brought within the pale of the Church by baptism, and it was hoped that after being so received many would in due course submit their hearts to the full power of the Gospel.

On the other hand, there were those from the very beginning who felt that a compromise was being made, and who were gravely disturbed at the admixture of worldly living that thus found its way into the Christian fellowship; nor indeed has there ever been a time from that day to this when a protest of this kind has not been strongly represented by some party within the Church.[2] There were the early monks or anchorites who believed that only in the greatest possible degree of withdrawal from the world's soiling touch could the true Christian life be lived, and whose own withdrawal could not but carry with it an adverse judgement upon their fellow Christians, however far they might be from affirming that these were called to live as they, and however devoutly these in their turn might revere them as having attained to a greater holiness. But there were also various movements towards the stricter discipline of the Church as a whole, movements which soon showed a sectarian and divisive tendency, and which were accordingly frowned upon by the majority of the bishops. Such were the Montanists (with Tertullian among them) from the second century onwards, the Novatians from the third, and the Donatists from the early years of the fourth. The Montanists regarded themselves (or some of their number) as prophets, and as entering the same kind of protest against the apostasy of the wider Church as the Hebrew prophets had made against the national community of Israel; they were a new faithful remnant, and their attitude to the bishops was not unlike the attitude of the Hebrew prophets towards the priestly tradition of an earlier day and place. After the official adoption of Christianity the monastic movement grew apace, but because its tendency was

[1] *De civitate dei*, xviii. 48–9.
[2] Cf. Rufus M. Jones, *The Remnant* (1920).

not on the whole sectarian or schismatic, the Church was able to absorb it into itself. This was done, as is well known, by the gradual recognition of a double standard of holiness, as it were an 'honours' and a 'pass' course, one for those living the monastic and the other for those living the secular life. The late Dr. Edwyn Bevan has given us a parable of curds and whey to illustrate this development, comparing it to 'the phenomenon of curdling, when instead of the milk having a uniform consistency right through, some of the constituents coagulate and leave the rest watery'.[1] Throughout the Dark Ages the problem was regularly solved on these lines, but in the latter part of the Middle Ages various sectarian protests began again to make their appearance, from the Waldensians down to the Lollards and Hussites and other precursors of the Reformation.

The Reformers themselves, as we have seen, united their sweeping condemnation of the worldliness of the Roman Church with the firm retention of the ideal of a Church that should embrace the whole community. Their aim was not the creation of a sect that would achieve purity by separating itself from the life of the community, but a thoroughgoing reform of the community itself. They thus attempted to unite the sectarian ideal with the ideal of a Christianized society.

'The Church of Calvinism', writes Troeltsch, 'is at once a "confessional" and a national Church, . . . and at once voluntary and compulsory, in that it takes for granted that all the elect will under adequate instruction open their ears to the Spirit of truth, while at the same time it demands that all the non-elect shall be suppressed to the glory of God and for the protection of the elect, and prevented from giving public expression either to their unbelief or to their wickedness.'[2]

This is exactly the difference between the English Puritans and, for example, the third-century Novatians, who also were spoken of as puritans ($\kappa\alpha\theta\alpha\rho\sigma\acute{\iota}$). The Reformation, however, was immediately followed by the appearance within Protestantism of sects which considered that the Reformers had left their work only half done. Prominent among these were the Anabaptists against whom Calvin so hotly contended in Geneva. Their name means 'the re-baptizers', for they insisted on baptizing again those who received the sacrament in infancy, and henceforward would baptize only adults of whose regeneration

---

[1] *Christianity*, p. 129.   [2] Op. cit., p. 729 f.

they were reasonably well assured. The later history of Protestantism is full of sectarian movements whose zeal for a stricter standard of church membership and church life led them to separate themselves from the great national Churches of the northern lands.

§

It remains to ask how far, in the successive periods we have surveyed, the pattern of general society was itself transformed by the inclusion of most or all of its members within the membership of the Church. As regards the period following the conversion of Constantine and Theodosius, this is an assessment which it is by no means easy to make. If we are to accept as genuine the documents quoted by Eusebius in his *Life of Constantine*, that emperor did cherish the hope of a real transformation. 'I knew', he writes in a letter, 'that if I should be able, in accordance with my prayers, to stabilize a common concord (*communem concordiam stabilire*) among all the worshippers of God, the administration of the commonwealth (*reipublicae administratio*) would also undergo a change congruent with the pious desires of all.'[1] In any case it is not without significance that such a purpose should have been attributed to him by a contemporary. How far the purpose was carried out either by himself or by his successors is another matter. Mr. Bevan ventures on the generalization that 'the new position which Christianity had acquired in the world made a greater difference to the character of Christianity than it did to the character of the world'.[2] Yet a certain difference even to the legislative structure of the commonwealth it did undoubtedly make. Certain laws were changed, and new ones added to their number. Many of these laws affected only the position of the Church; but a recent writer has studied the *Codex Theodosianus* and the *Corpus Iuris* of Justinian with intent to discover what other laws of Constantine and Justinian respectively bear the marks of Christian influence. His list for Constantine includes laws affecting the condition of the poor, the position of women, the treatment of slaves, the gladiatorial games, the treatment of prisoners, marriage and the family, the taking of usury &c. His list for Justinian includes laws affecting the treatment of

---

[1] *Vita Constantini*, ii. 65. [2] *Christianity*, p. 107.

slaves and freedmen, divorce and adultery, the punishment of
criminals, the ownership of property, the succession and inheri-
tance of children &c.[1] On the other hand, there was no thought
of working a radical change in the political or economic structure. The traditional configuration of society, with its institutions of private property, slavery, the hierarchy of classes, trade,
finance and military power, remained as it had always been.
St. Augustine, writing at the beginning of the fifth century,
still seems to take it for granted that on the whole the secular
life of the empire will go on its way unchanged, and his concern
is still mainly as to the right way of 'using' its advantages and
amenities. Yet though the Church did not aspire to change this
pattern, and was far from desiring to overthrow it, it continued
to bring its profound criticism to bear upon it, holding it subject
to God's ultimate condemnation. If it was the *remedium*, it was
also the *poena peccati*. As a punishment for our sins we had to
submit to an ordering of things that was itself sinful. But in
their vision of the heavenly future Christians had their own
transcendent ideal of a righteous society, and on the life of their
own monastic settlements this ideal could be more directly
brought to bear. Among the monks there was no private
property, no class distinction, no exchange (at least among
themselves) of filthy lucre, and no training for war; hence in
the monasteries men might see something of what a true Christian society might be like. If it is true, as a French historian
has said, that in the patristic period and throughout a great
part of the Middle Ages 'no books of devotion were composed
for Christians living "in the world"', because in those days
'all who proposed to take the quest for perfection seriously
became monks—either by retiring to the desert or cloister, or
by practising domestic asceticism of the monastic kind',[2] it is
the less surprising that equally little attention should have been
given to the reform of the world's political and economic
arrangements—or that, in Troeltsch's words, 'the conception
of a Christian civilization, of such a reordering of the common
life as would penetrate, mould, and renew the world, and with
it every conception of a social reform emanating from the

---

[1] J.Westbury-Jones, *Roman and Christian Imperialism* (1939), pp. 228 f., 246 ff.
[2] P. Pourrat, *La Spiritualité chrétienne*, vol. i, pp. 9–10, as quoted by K. E.
Kirk, *The Vision of God*, p. 359.

Church, was entirely absent'.[1] At the same time, there is no doubt that, as the generations passed, public opinion came to be more and more influenced by Christian standards. A new conscience about many things began to develop in the West. Humanitarian feelings of a new kind began to invade the public mind. Gradually also the cultural life was changed, as pagan gave place to Christian education, and pagan art and literature to a new Christian art and literature, however deeply these latter might be indebted in their turn to the existing Greek and Roman models.

The reconstruction of the Roman Empire by Charlemagne marks the beginning of a new era. Charlemagne's desire was to unite the West into a single homogeneous civilization, but this idea of a unity of civilization was a derivative from the unity of the Catholic Church, just as that was dependent upon the Christian teaching of the unity of God.[2] Moreover, the centre of this new civilization was no longer to be on the shores of the Mediterranean but in the lands of the northern barbarians. The required unity could therefore only be achieved if the work of evangelization and that of civilization went forward concurrently, just as in our own day they have gone forward concurrently in Africa and the Southern Seas. This is perhaps the fundamental reason why the Middle Ages mark the beginning of a new synthesis between Christianity and civilization.

'It was not', writes Troeltsch, 'any inward necessity or any conclusion arrived at by religious thinking that first compelled Christianity to develop a civilizing activity of this kind, or to bring under the dominance of ecclesiastical and religious ideas those spheres of life which were themselves not directly ecclesiastical in nature. It was rather the force of circumstance and the necessities of an uncivilized State, which had to use for its own purposes the Church's organisation and the still-living tradition of ancient civilization residing within it, and which could never, without such help, have succeeded in building up a civilization of its own. It was above all the genius of Charles the Great that pointed out this way and, in so doing, permanently determined the essential and characteristic foundations of Mediaeval Christendom.'[3]

[1] Op. cit., p. 126.
[2] Sir Ernest Barker quotes from Dante, *De monarchia*, i. viii: 'Ergo humanum genus bene se habet et optime, quando secundum quod potest Deo adsimilatur. Sed genus humanum maxime Deo adsimilatur, quando maxime est unum.'
[3] Op. cit., pp. 199 ff.

The Middle Ages thus represent the brave attempt to bring the whole of life under the control of Christian standards, yet it is important to realize the strictly limited way in which this task was conceived. The inevitability of the fundamental structure of existing society was accepted almost as completely as it had been in the early centuries; but while the early Church had perhaps put the main stress on its character as the sinful result of sin, Medievalism inclined rather to stress its character as embodying the will of God for the proper ordering of the secular activities of life. The Natural Law which governs the civil order is now more positively regarded as itself a Christian law, given for the use of those who have to live in the world, and therefore having its rightful place in the harmony of nature and grace. What was attempted, therefore, was not to exchange the existing social institutions for others but rather to permeate them more and more with a Christian spirit. Feudalism was Christianized: its fighting instincts were diverted to serve quasi-spiritual ends; its wars became crusades; its order of knighthood was consecrated to the defence of the widow, the fatherless and the oppressed; and its idea of honour was transmuted into chivalry. Similarly a brave attempt was made to regulate commercial transactions by Christian principle, to eliminate unearned profits and to substitute for competitive bargaining the principle of the fixed equitable price.[1] But there is still no trace of the idea, made so familiar to ourselves by the widespread revolt against the evils of the modern capitalistic order, of a radical recasting of the underlying social and economic structure.

This latter idea may appear equally remote from the Protestant thought of the Reformation period when considered as a whole, yet in Calvinism there is something of a closer approach to it. The holy community which Calvin sought to set up in Geneva represents in some ways a completer integration of Christianity with civilization than anything Europe had yet seen. It is true that there emerges within Calvinism, especially in its later Puritan developments, a more negative attitude to the cultural amenities than had been present in Medievalism, but just because this spirit of renunciation was not sealed off in

---

[1] Hudson and Reckitt, *The Church and the World*, vol. i, pp. 212–90, forms a useful introduction to the study of the social and economic teaching of the Middle Ages.

separate monastic communities but was extended to 'life in the world', the whole range of life was brought under the sway of radical Christian ideas to a greater extent than previously.

'To Calvin', Troeltsch writes again, 'the Church is not only a *Heilsanstalt* for the provision of the objective means of salvation; . . . it must at the same time be a *Heiligungsanstalt*, to busy itself with the Christianization of the whole life of the community, and to bring the whole range of life under the sway of Christian principles and purposes.[1] . . . Here then, for the first time in the history of Christian ethics, we have a conscious and, so far as the circumstances allowed, an all-inclusive Christian and ecclesiastical arrangement of society. Calvinism was Christian Socialism in the sense of a corporate configuration of the whole life of State and society, in the family and in the sphere of economics, in public and in private relations, to accord with Christian standards. It took thought that each individual should receive his appropriate share of the community's natural and spiritual possessions, and at the same time it sought to ensure that the whole of this Christian society should, in actual practice and in every detail, be an expression of the kingly rule of Christ.'[2]

In Calvin's idea, therefore, the economic aspect of the community's life was to be as subject as any other to the principles which he derived from the Bible. Nevertheless the application of this ideal was apparently not conceived as involving any very great interference with existing arrangements. Moreover, as time went on, and the complexity of modern life increased, the idea itself suffered change—if partly under the influence of a tendency that had been present in Calvinism from the beginning. The attempted sanctification of the economic life too often degenerated into a mere sanctioning of the existing structure. No doubt the part played by Calvinism and Puritanism in the origins of capitalism and its *laissez faire* has been considerably exaggerated by Max Weber[3] and others after him; for the same factors were at the same time at work in other places. I remember being both shocked and amused to see in the streets of Roman Catholic Lisbon the widely blazoned sign *Banco Espirito Santo e Commercial de Lisboa*; and though I afterwards learned that the 'Holy Spirit' was only the banker's surname, I was not wholly reassured. But Puritanism cannot be exonerated from the responsibility of compliance.

[1] Op. cit., p. 627.   [2] Ibid., p. 676.
[3] *Gesammelte Aufsätze zur Religionssoziologie*, vol. i, pp. 17–236.

Nevertheless the germinal idea of Christian social reform was here present, making it no accident that the modern movements in that direction should have principally made their appearance, and secured their following, within those lands which Calvinism has most deeply influenced. I believe also that the public life of these lands in times near to our own has approached closer to the true type of what I have called an open Christian civilization than that which has elsewhere been enjoyed. Its explicit renunciation of the ecclesiocratic or Hildebrandine ideal, its frank concession of a real autonomy to the various secular interests, its acceptance and indeed eager championship of the principle of religious freedom and, more generally, its complete conversion from the conception of a compulsive to that of an open Christian civilization, have, in spite of the new problems and perils which they have brought in their wake, turned out on the whole to be sources of increased solidarity and stability. Hence again it would appear to be no accident that in the present struggle for what Mr. Churchill called 'the survival of Christian civilization' the nations most indebted to the Calvinist tradition have proved themselves the most resolute of the peoples of the West.

II

THE CHRISTIAN ATTITUDE TOWARDS
CONTEMPORARY CIVILIZATION

SINCE the latter part of the eighteenth century there has developed within the frontiers of what is still called Christendom a situation new in the history of mankind, there being now millions of men and women in all our communities who profess no religious faith, take part in no religious observance, and have connexion with no religious institution. In addition to these are many more millions whose remaining links with the ancestral faith of their community have been reduced to a new minimum, there being some who seek the services of the Church only for the burial of their dead, while others desire to add to this only a Christian consecration of their marriage and perhaps Christian baptism for their infant children. It is true that when even the most detached among them sits down to write a letter, he still dates it from the year of Christ's birth and signs it with what he still speaks of as his Christian name—for the attempted abolition of the Christian calendar by the unbelieving Jacobins of 1792 met with little success at the time and has not been seriously suggested since. He also somewhat modifies his behaviour on that day of the week which commemorates Christ's resurrection and he feasts on those days of the year which commemorate His birth, His resurrection, and the descent of the Holy Spirit upon His disciples; days which he still speaks of as holidays, however far from his mind may be the original burden of that word. In these and countless other ways the print of Christ's hand is still upon the customary framework of his life, and we shall see later that it is also (much more than he usually suspects) upon the ideas in his mind; yet his general attitude is one of more or less complete detachment from the fellowship of Christian worship.

The causes of this situation are usually sought in the radical change which overtook so many of the acutest minds in Europe during the eighteenth century and which has prompted those most affected by it to speak of that period as the century of Enlightenment (*Illuminisme, Aufklärung*). Of course the new outlook has origins much farther back in the Renaissance and later Middle Ages, and it is to be found in a comparatively advanced form of development in not a few thinkers of the seventeenth century; but it was in the latter half of the eighteenth that it attained both its maturity and the beginning of its present widespread dissemination. The change amounts to the substitution of an entirely new mental *frame of reference* for that which Christianity had provided for the European mind during the previous fifteen hundred years. The essential ideas constituting this new frame are that the present world is an eminently satisfactory world—even perhaps, as Leibniz thought, 'the best of all possible worlds'; that human nature, too, is fundamentally good and capable of progressive improvement—even perhaps, as Condorcet and Godwin thought, to the extent of 'perfectibility'; that human society can be similarly improved or perfected; that a principal, if not the principal, means of such progress is the control, by means of the new empirical science, of the forces of nature; and that this control is possible because nature, instead of being subject to the special dispositions of Providence, is a uniform system conforming to invariable laws such as can be discovered by patient observation and experiment.

This system of co-ordinate ideas was not at first conceived in its entirety, hence it was not at first realized how radically it differed from the traditional Christian system or what an entirely changed mental and emotional setting it would, when completed, provide for all our thinking and living; and most of those who took an early part in the creation of it did not dissociate themselves from the Christian Church. Finally, however, the two outlooks, if taken in anything like their entirety, were felt to be fundamentally incompatible, and it is the sense of this incompatibility that lies at the root of those intellectual stresses and distresses which disturbed so many of the leading minds of the nineteenth century under the name of 'intellectual doubt'. From about the middle of the nineteenth century onwards considerable alleviation of this difficulty was provided by the growing recognition that certain important constituents of the new outlook, however completely absent they may have been from the Christian thought of earlier ages, were not only not incapable of being worked into the Christian system but even made for its further and very notable enrichment. It was moreover pointed out by some that these constituents were themselves indirectly Christian in inspiration. For however much the earlier phases of the Renaissance had seemed to mark a return from Christian traditions to those of pagan classicism, the new outlook which finally emerged from it was in some respects even more foreign to ancient Greek and Roman than it was to Christian ideas; since unlike paganism its hopes were set on the future and were in essence a sort of secularization (in the literal sense of transference to the earthly *saeculum*) of the Christian hope of eternal life; so that it is indeed difficult to imagine how the doctrine of earthly progress could have sprung up anywhere else than on soil prepared by the Christian Gospel. Nevertheless, when the new direction of thought was given its head, it found its way very easily into an intellectual climate very inhospitable to the fundamental Christian ideas and attitudes; and as this climate gradually extended itself throughout further areas of the community, an increasing detachment from Christian belief was bound to be the result.

I have, however, long been convinced that in determining the causes of our present situation full account must be taken not only of this disturbance of the traditional intellectual outlook but also of the simultaneous disturbance of the traditional social life of the community. The two disturbances are indeed inextricably intermingled in the later history of the eighteenth century, and especially in the ferment leading up to the French Revolution. The links uniting them are manifold, but none is more important than the progressive application to the people's industry of the scientific discoveries of the intellectuals. The increased control of nature lies at the root of both. When the doctrine of racial progress was first mooted it was *knowledge* that was believed to have progressed and to be capable of indefinite further progression, but the value of this was taken to lie mainly in the contributions it made to human happiness and comfort. Bury has noted that many of the earliest exponents of the doctrine—Cardan, Le Roy, Bacon and Campanella—single out three particular inventions as giving special point to their argument, namely, printing, gunpowder, and the mariner's compass.[1] But as time went on there was added to the progress

[1] *The Idea of Progress*, p. 54.

of knowledge the conception of social progress in the sense
with which we are now so familiar, and thenceforward, when
men spoke of progress, it was likely to be a different set of
technical inventions that prominently occupied their minds,
namely, the inventions associated with the Industrial Revolution, such as the steam-engine and the machines replacing the
hand-looms and spinning-wheels of the textile industries. These,
however, have turned out to be only the first precursors of
further inventions which have changed the whole pattern of
industrial life and the whole fabric of society as well as the face
of the land. A new definitive stage has been reached with the
invention of the conveyor-belt and all its derivatives. To-day
we live in a mass society such as the world has never before
seen—the Great Society, as Graham Wallas called it. The
essentially agrarian conditions of all previous ages, characterized
by small and almost self-supporting villages and compact little
towns of individual craftsmen and shopkeepers, has given place
to a huddled industrial life characterized by great factories,
workers' unions, mammoth cities, congested industrial areas,
chain and departmental stores, big business with its concen-
trated control of capital resources, and all the *Gleichschaltung*
associated with the influence of modern journalism, broad-
casting, and the cinema. The result has been to dispose the
population in entirely new ways. The primary groups of
family, neighbourhood, village, and country town have lost
their old cohesion and with it much of their old significance, and their place has largely been taken by groups
that must now be reckoned in hundreds of thousands and in
millions.

The effect on the traditional Christian outlook and habits
of the community has been immense. From the beginning the
family had been the primary unit of the Christian common life
and the primary agency for the transmission of the Christian
heritage, so that every threat to the integrity of family life is
necessarily at the same time a threat to the Church's influence.
Next to the family had come the parochial system, conforming
itself to the natural disposition of an agrarian population; but
as the social life of the parish has come to count for less and less,
the Church has found that this long-standing disposition of its
own resources (in man-power, buildings, and the like) no longer

tallies with the existing pattern of general society. In our own time the question is being raised whether this may not be rectified in a manner parallel to the earlier partial rectification of the intellectual maladjustment. As Christian faith has now worked certain elements of the modern outlook into its own texture, so cannot Christian order adapt itself to the modern community life? The answer, however, again seems to be that this can be done only to a limited extent. The Church can and must revise many parts of its existing organization; it must find its way into the new social groupings; it must go where the people are; and must, for instance, extend its appeal to the new radio and cinema audiences. Yet a limit is set to this most necessary reform by the doubt as to how far the spirit of Christian neighbourhood can ever be infused into the life of such an industrial society as now exists. For it would seem that the displacement of the primary by the wider social groupings is inevitably accompanied by a great and growing dissipation of the spirit of community itself. In fact it has yet to be shown that mass society, in anything like the form in which we now know it, is capable of developing *any* true sense of community, or that the chill impersonality of it can ever be spiritualized into a Christian togetherness with one's neighbours. The Church, for instance, can never accommodate itself to a social pattern which tends to the disintegration of the family and allows less and less opportunity for privacy and solitude, while at the same time frequently turning the next-door neighbour into a complete stranger; or to an industrial system which deprives the worker alike of the joy of labour and of any real sense of its dignity, cutting him off from nature in acquainting him only with a machine. It is surely not without significance that so many contemporary proposals for the political and economic organization of our mass society, in being hostile to the Christian faith, are at the same time hostile both to privacy and to the strengthening of family ties and find themselves very much at home with the machine and its mass-produced artifacts. My contention then is that the disturbance caused in the social life of Christendom by the Industrial Revolution is quite as potent a cause of the Church's changed situation as the disturbance caused in its intellectual life by the closely connected and roughly coeval movement known as the

Enlightenment.[1] For our religion has two sides to it. It is *pistis* and it is also *koinonia*. It is a faith and it is a fellowship. The two are inseparable parts of the same whole. And neither has ever flourished while the other has languished.

§

Very various views are taken as to how the Church should now respond to this situation. It is believed by many that the way of wisdom lies in the frank recognition of the Church's minority position within a society no longer Christian in any significant sense. Christian civilization, they say, has now become the shabbiest of fictions, and the illusion of its continued reality can have only a weakening effect on the Church's own life, blunting the sharp edge of its witness and encouraging compliance with worldly standards. The *corpus Christianum* of the Middle and Reformation Ages has, we are told, entirely disintegrated, and we have returned to the situation of the early Church, so that once again the master precept must be, 'Wherefore come out from among them, and be ye separate.'[2] There are others who go further and say—what, as we have seen, there had been somebody to say in almost every age—that such was always our situation, however much the Church's accommodation to worldly ideas prevented us from realizing it. The so-called triumph of the Church in the period of Constantine and Theodosius was on this view rather a declension. 'Thou hast conquered, O Galilean!' the last pagan emperor is reported to have said, as he died in battle on the Tigris; but it was the world that then conquered the Church rather than the Church the world. The *corpus Christianum* never was a reality; and some would add that it never can be such under terrestrial conditions. The apparently Christian complexion

[1] Cf. Karl Mannheim, *Diagnosis of our Time* (1943), p. 161: 'The psychological and moral crisis of our time is to a large extent due to the speed with which the industrial revolution built up its new organization, hardly leaving time to realize the psychological and moral implications of the changes it brought about. It has for long been obvious to the sociologist that if there is a clash between the principles of organization and the psychological needs of the individual, and if institutions do not succeed in enlisting the souls of men employed in them, then their emotions go sour and general restlessness prevents constructive development.'

[3] 2 Cor. vi. 17.

of general society was at all times only a camouflage, the very nature of the Gospel rendering it incapable of suffering this kind of dilution without entirely ceasing to be itself. What the Gospel does is to confront men with a clear-cut choice, in accordance with the words, 'He that is not with me is against me', and, 'I would that thou wert either cold or hot. So then because thou art lukewarm, and neither cold nor hot, I will spue thee out of my mouth.' The merely customary, and certainly the compulsory, Christian profession and observance of the so-called Ages of Faith was, therefore, on this view much more of a hindrance than a help to the fulfilment of the Church's mission in the world. One is reminded of the reply given by a certain Oxford don to a colleague who, in arguing for the continuance of compulsory attendance in the college chapel, suggested that compulsory religion was better than no religion at all. 'I am afraid', he is reported to have said, 'that my own mind is not sufficiently subtle to perceive the difference.' Thus there are those who welcome the new situation in which the Church finds itself, as clarifying an issue that has been confused for fifteen hundred years. And there are those more numerous who, while adopting a less negative attitude to the kind of permeation of community life by Christian ideas which characterized earlier ages, show only contempt for the more diffuse and residual influence which Christian ideas still exercise upon the public opinion and public life of our own day, considering this at least to be rather a liability than an asset to the Christian cause, as tending so to inoculate men with a mild form of Christian religiosity as to render them immune from the grand infection.[1] In a certain Clydeside town there is a sweetmeat factory where it is said that one may enjoy something of the taste of toffee by leaning over the boundary fence, yet even in these days of rationing there are those who prefer to wait for the rarer enjoyment of the real thing.

This way of thinking is by no means confined to a single theological school or ecclesiastical tradition. Even within the Roman Catholic Church there are apparently some to tell us

[1] This metaphor, often repeated, was first used by J. H. F. Peile in his Bampton Lectures on *The Reproach of the Gospel* (1907), p. 155 f.: '. . . by inoculating society at large with a very dilute and attenuated serum, secures for it a measure of immunity from violent and inconvenient attacks.'

that 'the Constantinian chapter' in the history of the West is
now definitely closed and who deprecate the attempt to reopen
it.[1] Still more are there those within Anglicanism, catholic and
high-church in temper and tracing their descent from one strain
of the Oxford Movement, who urge the Church to a much
franker recognition of its minority position in separation from
an increasingly pagan or merely secularist world, and who
would welcome the disestablishment of the Church of England
as one move in the resulting strategy.[2] 'All he did was to empty
the church', was the report given of the effect of one such
priest's arrival in a formerly latitudinarian parish; whereupon
another is said to have remarked, 'What a glorious work!'[3]
But it is in the Lutheran and Calvinist lands of continental
Europe that such views have hitherto been most strongly represented. Despite the general adherence of both Luther and
Calvin to the medieval ideal of the *corpus Christianum*, these
Reformers not only bitterly attacked the worldliness of the
medieval Church but were also well aware that the compromise,
of which this worldliness was the fruit, dated back to, and even
beyond, the days of the first Christian emperors. The Ritschlian movement in the German theology of the nineteenth century
developed a heightened awareness of and reaction against certain aspects of this compromise, namely, its alliance of Patristic
theology with the philosophy of pagan Greece, its transformation of primitive Church order under the influence of the social
and political structure of the pagan Roman Empire, and its
acceptance of the Greco-Roman *lex naturalis* as the basis of the
Church's adjustment to civilization. In our own century these
elements of Ritschlianism, together with several others, have
been inherited by those German and other continental theologians whom it is convenient, if a little unfair, to group together
under the general name of Barthian; and this in spite of their
bitter reaction from other and equally well-marked Ritschlian
tendencies such as do not directly concern us here. The Barthian
theologians have in their turn exercised a leading influence on
the recently developed Confessional Movement in the German

---

[1] *Vide* 't Hooft and Oldham, *The Church and its Function in Society*, p. 62.
[2] Cf. John Drewett, 'Diffused Christianity: Liability or Asset?' in *Theology*,
vol. xlv, no. 266 (August 1942).
[3] *Vide* Reckitt and Casserley, *The Vocation of England*, p. 143.

Protestant Churches, and it is within this movement that we find the strongest expressions of the minority position of the Church and the most outspoken repudiation of the idea of a Christian civilization. I shall content myself with quoting two sentences from a single writer, Dr. Günther Dehn. The first is this: 'We must learn to recognize that there is no one form of State life, of economics, or of any other social order, that is more in the Spirit of the Gospel than another'[1]—a position which forms a striking parallel to the declaration of the Ritschlian theologian, Wilhelm Herrmann, in a work published as early as 1879, that it is a matter of indifference for Christian faith whether metaphysics be leading us in a theistic, pantheistic, or materialistic direction.[2] And the other is this: 'Since Israel did not fulfil its God-given vocation to be God's Church as an entire nation, God's message is no longer addressed directly to the world, but to the elect.'[3]

This latter statement shows us exactly where such thinkers stand. They insist that the Church's position and strategy are permanently determined by the prophetic dissociation of the faithful remnant from the Israelite theocracy as a whole, and by its own early conception of itself as being continuous with this remnant. They are therefore renewing the protest which, as we have seen, has had its representatives in every age, against that movement towards a recovered theocracy, or at least towards a wider conception of the Church's destiny, which has prevailed throughout the whole of later Christian history.

For my own part I find it impossible to doubt that this protest has in large part been justified and has had its necessary place in the providential ordering of the life of each succeeding age. One can hardly imagine how the Church's history would read to-day if it had not been subjected to the constant criticism of the sects. Certainly the history of the Dark Ages would have made sorry reading if it had lacked the austere witness of monachism; while an even more important part has been played by the dissident movements from Montanism down to Methodism, as well as by various groups which, though not seceding from the national Churches, have fulfilled a like office within

---

[1] *Man and Revelation*, English translation, p. 157.
[2] *Die Religion im Verhältnis zum Welterkennen und zur Sittlichkeit*, p. 86.
[3] Op. cit., p. 142.

them. And in our own day we owe much to those prophetic voices which warn us that the Church, in seeking to maintain its alliance with a growingly secularist community, is in danger of growing itself more secular-minded. If it has always been difficult to be in the world without being also of it, the difficulty has never been greater than it is to-day. Never has the Christian doctrine of regeneration stood in more danger of neglect. Never have men more needed to be told that Christ prefers to have them cold than to have them lukewarm. Never have Christians more required to learn again, in groups however small, the true and original meaning of Christian togetherness in the communion of saints. Never has the Church had more need to be reminded that its first aspiration, no matter what kind of world it finds itself occupying, must be to become such a Church as its Lord desired to present to Himself, 'not having spot, or wrinkle, or any such thing'.[1]

Very great weight must therefore be given to the protesting movements of which I have spoken, and the Church is little likely to flourish if it fails to take up into itself a great part of the thought and feeling which they represent. Nevertheless I cannot think that they have the whole truth within their grasp. The question ultimately turns on the measure in which we believe the Church to have been justified in the principles governing its admissions to baptism in the various periods. And here I should lay the greatest possible stress on the distinction between what I have called the open Christian civilization of the modern period and the compulsive or conscriptive civilization that preceded it. It is only the former that any of us is likely to be found defending at this time of day. We are all firm believers in the principle of toleration which, though born of the indecisiveness of the wars of religion, and nourished in its youth by the success of the Protestant dissenting minorities in their struggle for independence, reached its maturity only in the admission of acknowledged unbelievers to the equal citizenship of the Western nations. None of us wishes to have the exercise of civil rights again associated with Church membership. None of us desires to return to an ecclesiastically dominated society. And however much we may long for a recovery of something of the unity that formerly pervaded all

[1] Eph. v. 27.

departments of life and thought, and a reconquest of what have been called the 'lost provinces' of our religion, we are equally concerned to retain for these a large part of the freedom they have gained and at least such a relative autonomy as was denied them by the compact medieval pattern of unity. Up to this point, then, I agree with Mr. Middleton Murry when he writes in his latest book that 'Whether we call the Church-inspired and Church-governed civilization of the Middle Ages a Christian civilization is of minor importance compared with the necessity of realizing, quite clearly, that that civilization has completely perished. It is no use trying to cling to scattered spars from the wreckage of that civilization.'[1]

But it has long seemed to me that the element of truth to which too little weight is given by the protesting movements is that contained in the Christian doctrine and practice of the baptism of families—a doctrine and practice which, very significantly, was a main target for the criticism of some of the more extreme of these movements, from Montanism to Anabaptism. The insight enshrined in this doctrine and practice is that the most likely way to bring men to an individual decision for Christ is to nurture them within a Christian community. This community is in the first place the family, and hence the controversy has always revolved round the baptism of infants born to Christian parents. But it is necessary that something of the same principle should be extended also to those larger social units in which, as the child grows to adolescence and manhood, he finds himself increasingly involved; and this is all the more necessary in a day like our own, when the family unfortunately counts for so much less in adolescent life than it used to do.

Just, therefore, as it is wrong to think meanly of the Christianity of children before they reach the age of personal decision and are confirmed in the faith, so I believe it wrong to hold as of no account the Christianity which pervades the life of a community before it is confirmed in the personal decision of every individual citizen. It is very evident, for instance, that Calvin's defence of paedobaptism and his championship of community religion were ultimately rooted in a single principle in his mind. While it was only to the children of baptized adults that he would administer baptism, this actually meant that he

[1] *Adam and Eve* (1944), p. 74.

administered it to all children, since 'to be a citizen of Geneva
it was necessary to make a profession of faith in Christ'.[1] Calvin
knew that many who made this profession were not truly re-
generate, and that many of the homes into which children were
born were therefore not truly Christian; and he taught that in
these cases baptism was unaccompanied by the promised bless-
ing; but he did not profess to know with anything like certainty
which or how many these cases were, and he was accordingly
not deterred from a practice which at least ensured that the
children of Christian parents should be adopted in earliest
infancy into the membership of the Church. It is, it seems to
me, by a legitimate extension of the same principle that Mr.
T. S. Eliot defines a Christian society as a society of 'men whose
Christianity is communal before being individual'.[2] This been
been the order of things throughout the whole of our Western
history and—as was so much stressed at the Tambaram Missionary Conference in 1938—it is the prevailing order in the
greater number of our mission fields to-day. Here are some
sentences from the report presented to the General Assembly
of the Church of Scotland by its Foreign Mission Committee
in 1941:

'The younger Churches are full of men and women whose evangelisa-
tion is far from complete. . . . They are converts in the sense that they
have turned from their old religion to submit themselves and their
children to the teaching and discipline which is offered in the Christian
name. . . . They value the help of the fellowship which they have
entered, and in simple ways they can carry a banner of witness for Him
whose name they have taken. But that they are awake to God in their
individual lives, that they know the forgiveness of their sins through
Christ, are leading an inward life of trust and obedience, and are con-
sciously drawing the strength of their daily lives from His grace, is simply
not true of the majority.'

Such words as these must give rise to grave disquiet in every
Christian breast, and they were written with no other intent
than to spur us on to a greater effort of evangelization, yet they
were far from being accompanied by the suggestion that the
problem can be solved by the immediate restriction of the

[1] L. B. Schenck, *The Presbyterian Doctrine of Children in the Covenant*
(Oxford University Press, 1940), p. 13.
[2] *The Idea of a Christian Society*, p. 59.

Church's membership to the minority 'to whom', as the report says, 'Christ is indeed a shining reality and who personally know Him and His redeeming work upon their lives', or to 'select companies of the twice-born'. For it is difficult to escape the conclusion that we Westerners owe the people of these missionary lands, not only the presence in their midst of such select companies, but also the provision of a Christian community life and a Christian culture to take the place of the indigenous life and culture which we have so rudely disturbed. The spread of Western civilization has everywhere shaken, and in many lands almost or quite destroyed, long-standing orders of society the secular aspects of which were closely integrated with the native religious cults. In most cases it has happened, and in many cases it has seemed inevitable, that the Christian missionaries themselves should combine the work of evangelizing with the work of civilizing. So inextricably were the native cults interwoven with the general habits and ideas of the people that together they had to remain or else together be changed. It was, as we have seen, the necessity of accompanying the evangelization of the barbarian lands of northern Europe with a parallel work of civilization that originally gave birth to the very conception of Christian civilization more than a thousand years ago; and now the same situation has repeated itself in respect of Asia and Africa and the islands of the Southern Seas. Can it possibly be our duty to offer to these peoples a Christian Church which guards its purity by restricting its numbers and confining itself to a narrowly conceived evangelism, *plus* a purely secular civilization? If not, it follows that the conception of a Christian civilization is something which it is still our duty to export.

It is, however, very much the same reason that I would put forward in favour of its domestic use. It is now long since the last effective vestiges of the indigenous religions of western and northern Europe were destroyed through the success of the Christian mission. Christianity has therefore a responsibility towards the general society of the West such as it would not have had if the old religions had retained their place in that society and their virility among those members of it who have not truly surrendered their hearts to Christ. For in such measure as the Church should now, by withdrawing into itself, seek to disclaim the regions of its more diffused influence, in that measure it would be abandoning the civilization of the West to a secularist condition which was, in part at least, the creation of its own earlier missionary activity.[1]

The case would no doubt have been somewhat different if the decline of Christian civilization during the last several centuries had been accompanied, not by a growing secularism and disappearance of all spirituality, but by a recrudescence of paganism or the appearance of a new religion. In Germany something like this has indeed recently happened, and the knowledge of this fact should incline us to a much more sympathetic understanding of the positions adopted by the leaders of the German Confessional Movement, and of such statements as I quoted above from a German theologian, than we might otherwise have accorded them. Small wonder that these persecuted brethren of ours should speak of being again in the situation of the early Church, of having to retire again into the catacombs, and of the ending of the era which began with Constantine! Moreover, we have all the more to learn from them, because we know how foolish it would be to assume that, as the saying is, 'It can't happen here'. For I take it as certain that if Christian ideas do not regain something of their former hold upon our national life, we shall sooner or later fall victim to such pagan ideas as have lately been resuscitated in Germany —and not in Germany alone. If the Spirit of Christ departs from the homes of the people, they will not long be found 'empty and swept and garnished', as so many of them are now, but evil spirits will enter in and either the old idols will be set up again or new ones fashioned. Yet I believe it equally the Church's duty to recognize that at least in Britain and America this stage has not yet been reached on any important scale. To that extent our situation differs from that of central Europe, and we must accordingly follow somewhat different counsels. For the fact that this stage has not been reached, and that even

[1] 'While the Wisdom of the East, the Law of Moses, and the Platonic Republic could offer the structure of the life without grace, Christendom cannot do so, because the forces which have done most violence to man's natural life —his man-centred thought and his arrogance in technique—have sprung from a perversion of energies released in Europe by the Christian religion.'—V. A. Demant in *Malvern 1941*.

those of our people whose working moral standards have become most completely detached from their Christian root are genuinely shocked by its appearance elsewhere, seems to me to provide the Church with an opportunity which may not again occur—an opportunity which the Church can grasp, not by retiring into itself as a self-conscious minority within the nation and separated from the great sweep of national life, but rather by endeavouring to strengthen the things that remain, building upon such diffused Christian sentiment as still exists in the public mind and not resting until this has been fortified into genuine Christian conviction.

It is sometimes said that in our own homeland the Church is once again faced with a fundamentally missionary situation and that its preaching to the people at home must therefore be of the kind it addresses to pagan races in far-away lands. This is, however, no more than a half-truth. Britain may be threatened with paganism, but it is not pagan yet, nor can I think that a wise strategy will address it as if it were. The word 'pagan' is often unthinkingly used as if it meant a man who was devoid of all religious sentiment and worshipped no gods. But all real pagans are full of religious sentiments and their fundamental error rather lies in worshipping too many gods. That is not our present error in this country. Such definite religious sentiment as continues to prevail among the masses of our own people is still Christian; and certainly such definite and positive standards as continue to prevail are at least more Christian than they are anything else. Many no longer regard themselves as Christians, but still less do they regard themselves as anything else that has sufficient substance in it to be given a name. The alternative they envisage is therefore not between being Christian and being pagan, but between being Christian and being nothing in particular; not between belonging to the Church and belonging to some rival spiritual community that claims an equally whole-hearted allegiance, but between belonging to the Church and belonging nowhere, giving no whole-hearted allegiance to anything. Such is the tragedy that has overtaken so much of our common life—that it belongs nowhere, has no spiritual home, no ultimate standards of reference, and little definite conception of the direction in which it desires to move.

That has been cu..

§

It will thus be seen how largely I am in agreement with
Mr. Eliot's understanding of the present situation in his book
on *The Idea of a Christian Society*.

'A society has not ceased to be Christian', he writes, 'until it has
become positively something else. It is my contention that we have
to-day a culture which is mainly negative, but which, so far as it is
positive, is still Christian. I do not think that it can remain negative,
because a negative culture has ceased to be efficient in a world where
economic as well as spiritual forces are proving the efficacy of cultures
which, even when pagan, are positive; and I believe the choice before
us is between the formation of a new Christian culture, and the acceptance of a pagan one. Both involve radical changes; but I believe that
the majority of us, if we could be faced immediately with all the changes
which will only be accomplished in several generations, would prefer
Christianity.'[1]

It is this preference that seems to me so important a fact and
also, if only it can be turned to good account before it further
weakens, so real an asset. For myself, I continue to thank God
that I was born not only into a Christian family which represented to me the Christian Church in microcosm, but also into
a civilization whose laws, manners, and public standards had
at least been deeply affected by the impact of Christian truth;
and I cling to what is left of this civilization, believing the hope
of the future to lie in such a reinvigoration of it as can result
only from its regained hold upon the fundamental Christian
ideas. If this hope should be disappointed, the Christian would
still be in secure possession of that eternal hope which must
ever be his soul's chief anchor; but willingly to surrender the
lesser hope, while there remained a prospect of its being in
some measure fulfilled, would be sadly to constrict the possibilities of his earthly walk and conversation. It would also
involve a perilous prospect for his children; for if these, though
born into a Christian home, are to be educated in spiritually
neutral schools and then launched into a spiritually neutral
society fed by neutral newspapers and a neutral B.B.C.,
how many of them will be strong enough to swim against the
tide? Against the danger of their being so inoculated with a

[1] Op. cit., p. 13.

milder communal Christianity as to be rendered immune from
the onset of a more personal conviction, I cannot but set this
other and greater danger. And I set against it also the very
different danger that their Christianity should degenerate under
such a pressure into a form of self-righteousness, since it is
unfortunately true that very many of the efforts to form a 'pure'
Church in the greatest possible degree of separation from the
world, whether as an *ecclesiola in ecclesia* or as an *ecclesiola extra
ecclesiam*, have been dogged by the temptation to pharisaism.
Even those who endeavour to put their trust in divine forgiveness rather than in their own greater worthiness are likely, in
such circumstances, to construct a new edifice of spiritual pride
out of the consciousness of their own election to grace.

Such a recovered Christian civilization would clearly be of
the open type which alone I am prepared to defend, and in it
the older conscriptive idea of the Church's authority would
have completely given place to the idea of religious freedom.
A Christian society of this kind would therefore be both more
and less than a society of Christians. It would be more, because
it would be Christian in the impersonal configuration of its life
and not merely in the individual dispositions of its members.
It would be less, because not all its members would necessarily
be Christian in their individual dispositions. This is, I think,
exactly Mr. Eliot's conception. 'What the rulers believed', he
writes concerning such a society, 'would be less important than
the beliefs to which they would be obliged to conform. And
a skeptical or indifferent statesman, working within a Christian
frame, might be more effective than a devout Christian statesman obliged to conform to a secular frame. For he would be
obliged to design his policy for the government of a Christian
society.'[1] And again, 'It is not primarily the Christianity of
statesmen that matters, but their being confined, by the temper
and traditions of the people which they rule, to a Christian
framework within which to realise their ambitions and advance
the prosperity and prestige of the country.'[2]

Not very different is the outline of a Christian society traced
by M. Maritain in his book on what he calls 'integral humanism'.

'The positive pole of its direction', he writes, 'would be integral

[1] Op. cit., p. 28.   [2] Op. cit., p. 27.

Christianity, the various degrees which are more or less remote or diverted from this end being ordered according to its political wisdom. Thus the commonwealth would be vitally Christian, and the various non-Christian spiritual groups included in it would enjoy a just liberty. . . . Such a temporal unity will not be, as was the consecrational unity of mediaeval Christendom, a maximal unity: it will be, on the contrary, minimal, its core of formation and organization in the life of the person not being on the highest level of the latter's supra-temporal interests, but on the plane of the temporal itself. It is for this reason that this temporal or cultural unity does not *in itself* require a unity of faith and religion, and that it can be Christian while including non-Christians in its circle. . . . It is not to the search for a theoretic common minimum, it is to the effectuation of a common task that all are called, believers and unbelievers. . . . This common task . . . is not consecrationally but *secularly* Christian' and hence 'does not in the least demand in its beginning a profession of faith in the whole of Christianity from each man. On the contrary, it includes in its characteristic features a pluralism which makes possible the *convivium* of Christians and non-Christians in the temporal city.'

This writer therefore draws a clear distinction 'between political activity as exercised by Christians and political activity as inspired by Christian principles'. The latter activity, he says, 'does not need all Christians, nor only Christians: but only those Christians who have a certain philosophy of the world, of society and of modern history; and such non-Christians as recognize more or less completely the cogency of this philosophy'. Nevertheless, according to M. Maritain, such a conception presupposes 'that those who take the initiative will be Christians, with a full and total comprehension of the end to be attained', though in this region of social and political activity 'it is the normal course of things that the initiative should come from below', that is, not from the courts of the Church nor yet from those in holy orders, but 'from laymen acting at their own risk and peril'.[1]

M. Maritain is a Roman and Mr. Eliot an Anglo-Catholic; yet I, who am a Presbyterian, find myself in sufficient general agreement with this common direction of their thought to allow their words to stand in this place without further comment of my own.

---

[1] *True Humanism* (English translation of *L'Humanisme intégral*), pp. 161, 166, 200, 259, 401, 265.

III

THE FUTURE OF THE WEST

MR. H. G. WELLS will not be suspected of being a prejudiced witness for the defence of Christian civilization, yet in his *Outline of History* he writes as follows of the western Europe which, shortly after the death of Hildebrand, was about to enter on the First Crusade.

'There is everywhere a common belief, a linking idea, to which men may devote themselves, and by which they can co-operate together in a universal enterprise. We realise that, in spite of much weakness and intellectual and moral unsoundness, to this extent the Christian Church has *worked*. . . . Here for the first time we discover Europe with an idea and a soul! Here is a universal response of indignation at the story of a remote wrong, a swift understanding of a common cause for rich and poor alike. You cannot imagine this thing happening in the empire of Augustus Caesar, or indeed in any previous state of the world's history. . . . It is clear that we are dealing with something new that has come into the world, a new clear connection of the common interest with the consciousness of the common man. . . . The beginning of the Crusades displays all Europe saturated with a naive Christianity.'[1]

It is important, however, that we should clear our minds as to the precise nature of this saturation, and of this 'diffused Christianity', which was to continue as characteristic of the West down almost to our own time. Both by the sceptical critics of our faith and by the radical Christian critics of our civilization it is sometimes said to have been no more than a façade, an outward profession of piety camouflaging an essential worldliness. True Christians, it is said, have always and everywhere been but a small minority, and the change that has now overtaken us is not that the number of Christians has diminished, but that non-Christians no longer find it necessary to wear the Christian disguise. I constantly find myself reading statements to this general effect, but I am never able to read them without feeling that they are unhistorical and miss an important part of the truth. There is, of course, no doubt that in every period *some* Christian profession was mere pretence and 'eye-wash', covering either total scepticism regarding the Church's

[1] Bk. VI, ch. xxxiii, §§ 9, 11.

dogmatic teaching or a total flaunting of its moral standards; yet even here it must be said that public opinion counted at all times for much more than legal compulsion in the maintenance of conformity. 'The quiet tyranny of custom', writes Dr. Coulton, 'is often more repressive than the law and the police, and even more operative in reaction upon the rebel's mind than in action upon the conformist's.'[1] The powerful encouragement of Christian profession by public opinion preceded by many centuries the legal enforcement of it, and was always the real power behind such enforcement; and again it was the change of public opinion that brought about the relaxation of enforcement within our modern states—and not vice versa. The most important fact about the ages of conformity, therefore, is not that Christianity was then established by law but that it was then favoured by public opinion. How much did this favour amount to? It certainly did not mean that all who shared it were true Christians, that they had surrendered their hearts to the power of the Gospel and were in possession of the deep inward secret of Christian joy and peace. Did it then mean no more than that for conventional reasons, because it was the fashion of their social superiors, or because uniformity was necessary to the health of the body politic, they were willing to observe the Church's ordinances? Is it only thus that civilization was ever Christian? There are those who speak as if this were all, but it is certain that they speak hastily and unthinkingly; for they omit from their reckoning the all-important fact, so truly grasped by Mr. Wells, that there was 'everywhere a common belief, a linking idea'.

Here undoubtedly is to be found the constitutive element of Christian civilization—in the fact that the population as a whole *believed* what the Church taught. There were isolated intellectuals who questioned it in their hearts, but the immense majority of men was beyond the reach of doubt. The Christian view of man, the world and God, formed the unquestioned background of their minds and provided the framework within which their lives were lived. However naïvely understood, however corrupted by pagan and superstitious admixtures, it was at least all they had. However grossly many of them may have neglected the observances it imposed, however shame-

[1] *Fourscore Years*, p. 99.

lessly they may have acted in despite of its moral standards,
they did not doubt the authority of these standards or the right-
fulness of these observances, and they understood well enough
that in failing to conform to them they were doing wrong. These
were the days, as we might say, when even the devils believed
and trembled. Now I need hardly remind you that St. James
speaks with considerable contempt of this kind of belief which
is shared even by the devils, making them tremble in their
devilry without apparently prompting them to desist from it;
nor need I remind you how careful the Church has always been
to distinguish it from that *fides salvifica* which is a whole-hearted
trust in the God and Father of our Lord Jesus Christ. So long
as a man's belief in God does no more than make his hand shake
as he sets it to the foul deed, or give him a faintly painful twinge
of conscience as he takes the next step in his downward course,
it is obviously doing him no good at all. Nevertheless his
twinge and tremor bear witness to the mark that Christian
truth has made upon his mind, and still more eloquent witness
to the mark it has made on the general mind of the society in
which he lives. The Christian civilization of the past has not
then been a civilization all or even most of whose members had
come under such a saving conviction of Christian truth as to
work renewal in their inward man, leading them to observe in
all things the Christian standards of conduct. It was rather a
civilization in which nearly all acknowledged the authority both
of that truth and of these standards, accepting in their minds
even what they delayed to take to heart, and trembling when
they were farthest from obeying.

'Thou believest that there is *one* God', says St. James before
adding drily, 'thou doest well: the devils also believe, and
tremble.'[1] But while the unity of God was thus taken for
granted by everybody, and even (as was supposed) by the evil
spirits (τὰ δαιμόνια), in the Palestinian world which this writer is
believed by most scholars to have been addressing, it was all
but completely new to that Western world to which the Gospel
had been carried by St. Paul. And I believe it is difficult to over-
estimate the extent to which this Christian belief, with its
necessary corollaries of the unity of nature and the unity of man,
lies at the base of later European civilization.

[1] James ii. 19.

Having now cleared our minds as to the sense in which the civilization of our forefathers may be called Christian, let us try to clear them also as to the residual sense in which our present society may be held to merit such a name. It is evident that 'the common belief, the linking idea', of which Mr. Wells spoke, has lost much of its former hold. Modern life is no longer carried on within the setting of the Christian world-view, but either is a pragmatic business lacking any general setting, or attempts to conform itself to a new complex of ruling ideas having their centre in the dogma of racial progress. With the common belief has gone the common worship, and with the common worship much of the community life of which it formed the natural focus—though I notice that Dr. Coulton claims that 'In any English village, the official incumbent still forms the natural nucleus of crystallization for all idealisms and healthy activities, except in that tiny minority of cases where his personal failings reduce him to a negative factor.'[1] Is it then that, even when the belief has grown dim and the worship fallen into neglect, our morals are still Christian? Few things, I think, are more difficult to generalize about than the moral practice of any period, and not least of one's own period. There are respects in which present moral practice in a country like our own compares favourably with that of earlier centuries, and there are also very obvious respects in which it marks a sad decline; but I should myself venture the judgement that the former concern those virtues which are not specifically due to Christian influence, while the latter concern the virtues with whose growth in the Western world Christianity had a very great deal to do. And no doubt, as Canon Peter Green says in his recent pamphlet on *The Moral Condition of Great Britain To-day*, 'the reason is plain. Having disestablished the first four of the Ten Commandments we have robbed the last six of all validity.'[2] We cannot then say that our moral practice gives us the right to think of our present society as Christian, but I believe the case to be different when we turn our attention to our *professed moral standards*. So far as our civilization is still Christian, it is this principally in respect of the fact that its *conscience* is still recognizably Christian, that we judge other men and nations, and to a less extent allow ourselves to be

[1] *Fourscore Years*, p. 299.   [2] Op. cit., p. 19.

judged, by norms of conduct which Christianity introduced into the world. When men are asked what they conceive themselves to be defending in the war against the Nazis and the Japanese, they will nearly always mention principles which can be shown to have formed themselves in the mind of the West as the result of Christian influence. Here lies the true meaning of Mr. Churchill's assertion that upon the Battle of Britain depended the survival of Christian civilization.

When our forefathers spoke, as they frequently did, of the 'diffused Christianity' that pervaded the *corpus Christianum* of the West, they meant that, while not all were of 'the elect', or were enjoying the inward blessings of the Gospel, yet all implicitly acknowledged the truth of the Christian creed, the duty of Christian worship, and the authority of the Christian standards of conduct. That, for instance, was what Thomas Chalmers meant when he used the phrase in 1832 in defending the principle of Establishment: 'I hold the Establishment to be not only a great Christian good, but one indispensable to the upholding of a diffused Christianity throughout the land.'[1] But when we use the phrase to-day we think only of the surviving influence of Christian moral ideals after the impulse of worship has failed and the belief grown dim and shadowy. 'I am not a Christian', writes Professor Gilbert Murray in his recent Conway Lecture—yet goes on at once to declare his belief in what he calls 'the precious quality of Christian civilization'.[2]

Professor Murray is well aware that what divides his own outlook from that of former ages is that, while retaining the ideals, he has surrendered the supporting belief. This belief is to him a 'myth'—the Christian myth; and he argues that the ideals must now make shift to survive without this mythical support. When he is asked what other support he can find for them, what other reasons he can adduce for their obligatoriness, he has only this to say: 'I, if I am questioned, answer hesitatingly in terms of the result of long human experience, with some stress on evolution and the social and gregarious instincts, conscious all the time that my explanation is not fully adequate, but content in my heart to admit that, though deeply interested in all such

[1] Hanna, *Life of Chalmers*, vol. iii, p. 266: quoted by Hugh Watt, *Thomas Chalmers and the Disruption*, p. 94.
[2] *Myths and Ethics* (1944), p. 28.

attempts at explanation, I do not base my faith on their scientific correctness.'[1]

But Professor Murray must do better than that if he is to ensure the survival of the ideals which he has so valiantly championed throughout the whole of a long life. Here is only vague and jumbled reference to three forlorn attempts that were made during the course of the eighteenth and nineteenth centuries to find some non-Christian foundation for Christian moral standards—the pragmatic, evolutionist, and 'moral instinct' varieties of empiricist ethics. Professor Murray is, so far as my knowledge extends, the first to try to hold them all together; and each one of them, when taken separately, has been effectively torn to shreds even by those philosophic critics who were not themselves writing from a Christian point of view. The support which Professor Murray proposes for his ideals is therefore mythical enough in the popular sense of that much-abused word. It is a myth that the validity of moral standards can be established by observation of their consequences in action; it is another myth that it can be established by appeal to animal instincts; it is a third myth that the biological theory of evolution does anything to prove it; and the three together form a striking example of mythological syncretism.

Yet they do this, as I readily admit, only in the debased meaning of the word. A real myth is a fanciful picture which attempts to find for ideals a background in reality, whereas Dr. Murray's myth is rather a fanciful attempt to dispense with such a background. I am convinced, however, that this latter must always be a forlorn hope. 'Values', writes Dr. Hocking of Harvard, '... can survive only if, reaching out towards a metaphysical condition which their dream-shapes foreshadow, they *find it*. They need reality to climb on; they need a reality they can climb on. They want an independent source of standards, a mooring outside nature.'[2] Dr. Murray has surrendered the Christian conception of reality, but he clings—nobody more gallantly—to the ideals and the civilization which are the historical fruit of that conception. He is of a generation—in many ways a noble generation—which desperately desired to call halt *at that point* to a dissipation of the Christian outlook which up

[1] *Myths and Ethics* (1944), p. 29.
[2] *Human Nature and Its Remaking*, p. 412.

to that point they had done everything in their power to encourage. He is of the spiritual generation of the George Eliot who, walking with Frederick Myers in the Fellows' Garden of Trinity College, Cambridge, 'on an evening of rainy May', 'taking as her text . . . the words God, Immortality, Duty, pronounced with terrible earnestness how inconceivable was the first, how unbelievable the second, and yet how peremptory and absolute the third'.[1] He is of the spiritual lineage of the James Anthony Froude who wrote that 'Opinions alter, manners change, creeds rise and fall, but the moral law is written on the tablets of eternity. For every false word or unrighteous deed, for cruelty and oppression, for lust or vanity, the price has to be paid at last: not always by the chief offenders, but paid by some one. Justice and truth alone endure and live. Injustice and falsehood may be long-lived, but doomsday comes at last to them. . . .'[2] But the generation now rising begins to know that to speak thus is to cry for the moon. The forces now unleashed against the ideals of Christian civilization are far too mighty to be stayed and overthrown by so flimsy a defence. These forces have myths of their own, faked myths perhaps and certainly most pernicious ones, but more likely, I fear, to be effective than Dr. Murray's. I therefore fasten very eagerly on Dr. Murray's confessed awareness that his explanation is not fully adequate and that he does not base his faith on its scientific correctness; and am disappointed only that he has not inquired, or has not enlightened us, as to this deeper basis of his faith. For what can this basis be but a belief about *reality*? And if it is called in to support *Christian* ideals, how can it be expected to play its part effectively unless it be a *Christian* belief about reality?

§

It is unlikely, then, that the Christian conscience of the West can long survive its present disseverance from its original setting of belief and its original nourishment of worship. There must either be some return to the integrity of the Christian outlook or a still further disintegration. The German Romanist philosopher, Dr. Peter Wust, has written eloquently of the

[1] F. W. H. Myers, *Modern Essays*, p. 269.
[2] *Short Studies in Great Subjects*, vol. i, 'The Science of History'.

'metaphysical terror' which he discerns behind the apparent complacency of recent Western civilization; but more recently still there have been many symptoms of what I might call a metaphysical hunger. A generation long accustomed to be fed on the ideal begins again its quest for the real. And here, if anywhere, I hold our hope to lie. For only thus can the West again come to understand that what Christianity did was not to set before men new ideals, a new moral code, a new system of ethics, or a new law to replace the old, but rather to give them a new conception of reality, a new access to reality, and a new assurance of the grace of God, from whom all reality proceeds; and that therefore, while indeed there is a Christian ideal and a Christian ethic, the secret of obedience to them lies in the humility engendered by the knowledge that we must trust for our ultimate salvation not to the measure of our own goodness but to the unmeasured divine forgiveness of our sin. 'I simply want to ask you one thing,' St. Paul would say to our generation, as he said long ago to the Galatians; 'did you receive the Spirit by doing what the Law commands or by believing the Gospel message?'[1]

This is something that was well understood by former ages. Both the medieval and the Puritan worlds were dominated by the sense that

> yonder all before us lie
> Deserts of vast eternity.[2]

They knew that our earthly existence was not primarily of value for its own sake, but only as the forecourt of a greater glory yet to be. And even the Renaissance, however much it desired to find an independent value in the things of time, was not on the whole minded to question the greater claim of the interests of eternity. This does not mean that even in the Middle Ages or in the holy communities of Puritanism the generality of men acted according to this belief; on the contrary not even the saints of these periods would have claimed for themselves that they had acted up to its full implications. What it means is that this belief held the minds of all serious thinkers, and of almost all men in their most serious thought. There is a sense, then, in which the ages to whom we owe our Christian civiliza-

---

[1] Gal. iii. 2; Moffatt's translation.
[2] Andrew Marvell, *To His Coy Mistress*.

tion valued that civilization less highly than we are inclined to
do to-day. They valued it indeed, but gave it only a secondary
place. It may almost be said to have come into being as a
by-product of something immeasurably more to be treasured.
'If that age was an age of faith,' writes Mr. Christopher Daw-
son, it is because the men of that age 'put their trust in
something more than civilization, and something outside
history.'[1] And of the modern shift from this point of view
Dr. Peter Wust writes that:

'Whereas, in the best periods of the Middle Ages and of antiquity,
the cultural development is, so to speak, the automatic result of a life
steeped in the liturgical consecration of religion—natural in antiquity,
natural-supernatural in the Middle Ages—, at this point the centre of
gravity is suddenly and fatally shifted. The cultural achievement becomes the primary consideration, the sanctity of religious fellowship and
the life of faith of secondary importance. Already in antiquity we find
this change of gravity in the transition from Aeschylus to Euripides. For
Aeschylus dramatic art was still part of a liturgical life; for Euripides it
had already become an end in itself.'[2]

Something of this weakness has been in danger of pervading
the present remarkable discussion concerning the future of
education in our own land, giving rise in some Christian minds
to the fear that their religion was being valued less for its own
sake than for its stabilizing influence upon general society.
Yet, if we are to be fair, we must remember that when statesmen
speak *as statesmen*, a certain variation of emphasis is here both
natural and legitimate. And certainly the unanimity of their
recent utterances has been very impressive. I shall take time
to quote from three such utterances. In the report, presented in
1943, of the Committee of the Secondary School Examina-
tions Council appointed by the Board of Education in 1941, we
read as follows:

'There is an illusion . . . that we have suddenly become a nation of
unbelievers, and that two or three generations ago we were thoroughly
Christian. But no one who weighs the evidence of history in this or
any other country can suppose that the political and economic systems
have ever been effectively Christian; indeed it is a common cry to-day
that Christianity cannot be called a failure because it has never been

[1] *The Making of Europe*, p. xix.
[2] *Crisis in the West*, English translation, p. 19.

tried, and there exists an almost instinctive desire, particularly among the young, that it shall be tried both within and between the nations, and in no formal and conventional manner. This is an element of real promise for the future, and it is the foundation of the present genuine demand that there shall be an opportunity for religious education in all schools.'[1]

It is with a little more hesitation that I quote from the report, published in 1942, of the Conservative Sub-Committee on Education, because some have found in it a tendency towards the danger to which I have referred; but among other things it says this:

'Is it the business of the State to concern itself at all with religion? . . . That is, in fact, the question which now needs to be isolated and answered, before the State can begin to know what it is doing, whenever its policy —in the educational or any other field—touches religion. So far as we are aware it has not only not been answered by any modern political party but has been perpetually pushed out of sight and remembrance, lest the answer might add difficulty to the complex practical problems which have come to constitute the main business of British statesmanship. In our submission the truth is the other way round. If the general question can be answered, the solution of these practical problems will be made easier. We believe that the general question *can* be answered; and that whether it is regarded from a long-ranging or a short-ranging viewpoint, it is a question of deep and indeed vital importance to the whole community.'

And one of the conclusions reached in the report is that

'Every possible opportunity, encouragement and assistance must be given by the State for the effective training of every child in the religious principles approved by its parents or guardian, provided that such training is not hostile to the State. Where such training is not available, the State must provide the most effective undenominational Christian training it can.'[2]

Finally, in the report presented in 1943 by the Youth Advisory Council appointed by the Board of Education in the previous year, we read as follows:

'We are concerned to see preserved, or born, a genuinely Christian civilization. This we take to mean, not a civilization all of whose members are necessarily professing Christians, but one in which the Christian belief in God, and all that is consequent upon it of human liberty and

---

[1] *Curriculum and Examination in Secondary Schools*, p. 84.
[2] *Looking Ahead: Educational Aims*, pp. 19, 38.

brotherhood, and the preservation of the fundamental ideas of truth, goodness and beauty, set the tone for society.'[1]

It will be seen how closely this conception of a Christian civilization resembles that which I have myself ventured to defend, and I must confess to finding it a most encouraging sign of the times that there should be this widespread returning consciousness both of its essential nature and of its very great value.

§

Nevertheless, when the full light of the Gospel is cast upon it, all earthly civilization, including that which has been most permeated by Christian influence, becomes subject to ultimate criticism as falling under the final judgement of God. A society which has a 'Christian tone' without being completely Christian in substance, though it may represent the best attainable in a world of sin, is clearly not a conception in which the mind can rest. It is what M. Maritain calls an *ambivalent* conception. Such an earthly city, he says, is no realization of the divine ideal, but only a kind of refraction of it. Yet because it is a refraction of the true light, and because no full realization is possible in a fallen world, Christian criticism must, as I have already argued, never be pushed to the extreme of disengagement from its problems. Least of all in our own time is it permissible for Christians to adopt such an attitude. The ills of our present social order are such that the Christian who refused to interest himself in the mending of them could at best salve his conscience by retiring into a monastery, and the Church by withdrawing 'into the catacombs' of a small-scale social order of its own making. That too would be an evasion of duty, but an evasion of a less offensive kind than that involved in complacently accepting the amenities, and availing ourselves of the privileges, of a society which continues to dispense its privileges and amenities in a cruelly unjust way, so that others are necessarily debarred from much that we ourselves enjoy. Christians who to-day defend the Church's slowness to concern itself with social reform by standing fast on the distinction between 'religion and politics', or between 'religion and economics', too often find themselves in the same camp as those men of the world whose opposition to projected reforms proceeds only

[1] *The Youth Service after the War*, p. 11.

from the defence of their own vested interests in the existing order.[1] Such a clean-cut discrimination of the religious sphere from the economic and political may have served a useful purpose in former orders of society; within Medievalism where pope and emperor represented parallel functions of a single, and withal a Christian, society; or even within the liberalism of Victorian Britain where a single general mind prevailed among the leaders of both Church and State, so that the discrimination in question hardly meant more than a natural division of labour. But as the society of the West has become less and less Christian, what was once only a division of labour has of necessity grown more and more into a conflict of principle.

Hardly more tenable, though not infrequently put forward, is the view that the Church's criticism of the social order must confine itself to a merely negative role. The Church, it is said, must expose the injustices of the existing order, and must vigorously protest against them, but is not called upon to point the way to better alternatives. This, however, is to condemn the Church to the most thankless of all tasks—to the task of attempting to destroy what it will not help rebuild, raising a carping voice where it stretches out no guiding hand. It would, no doubt, be an equally grave disaster, were the Church so to concern itself with the detail of political and economic arrangements as to become a party in the State or to align itself with a particular party programme; for party government is of the essence of the liberal order, and, while anything of that remains, the distinction between the spheres of religion and politics must retain a large measure of validity. Fortunately, however, those who so advise us are few. The imminent danger is not in that direction, but is rather the danger that, by allowing the political and economic order to take care of itself, the Church of Christ will tragically fall short of its duty of bringing the light of the Christian Gospel to bear upon every activity of the common life.[2]

[1] A certain parallel may be found in the words of Graham Wallas, *The Great Society* (1914), p. 374: 'In England to-day Mr. Belloc and Mr. Chesterton, while attempting to re-create the ideal of Catholic peasant-proprietorship, too often find themselves in alliance with those interests which have no ideals beyond the rapid making of large fortunes.'

[2] I may here be allowed to remark that I am not in these lectures concerning myself with the relations between Church and *State*, and especially not with the

Nevertheless, as I have said, even the most Christianized of earthly civilizations is seen by Christian faith to fall under the ultimate judgement of God. For however strenuously we may oppose Ranke's use of the fact that every moment of temporal history is equidistant from eternity, and the consequent doctrine, represented in the words already quoted from Dr. Dehn, that no one form of social or cultural order is nearer to the Kingdom of God than any other, it still remains true that even the nearest form is very far away. 'True justice does not exist', wrote St. Augustine, 'save in that republic whose founder and ruler is Christ—if we choose to call it a *respublica* on the ground that it is undeniably a *res populi*.'[1] St. Augustine was no doubt unduly pessimistic in his estimate of earthly possibilities, but the reason he proposes for his assertion that the Christian can never offer more than a qualified loyalty or attachment to any earthly civilization remains as valid as ever. It is that every earthly civilization is a civilization largely corrupted by sin, and that the only justice it knows is therefore the kind of justice which can exist in a society of men who remain largely unjust in their own individual desires. This insight is represented throughout almost the whole history of the Church by the distinction, already implicit in the thought of St. Augustine's predecessors and remaining in general currency until long after the close of the Middle Ages, between what may best be called (in the convenient terminology made familiar to us by Troeltsch) the absolute and the relative Law of Nature. The prior and simpler distinction between the various systems of positive law which were in use in different nations, and the Natural Law which was the foundation of them all as well as the criterion by which the justice of each must be appraised, had already been taken over by Christian from pagan thought, the Natural Law being identified with the Divine Law given through Moses. But now it is seen that this Divine Law of Nature was a law adapted to the conditions of a sinful world; and does not therefore represent either God's original or His ultimate design for human living, as represented respectively in the conceptions of

desirability or otherwise of the statutory establishment of one branch of the Church by the State. My concern is with the relation of Christianity, and of the Churches, to the *community*; of which the State, except when it is totalitarian, represents only one function.   [1] *De civitate dei*, ii. 21.

a Primitive State before the Fall and of a final Kingdom of
Heaven after the close of history. In that design there is no
place for force or compulsion; for penal action or any kind of
restraint; for distinctions of master and servant, or of rich and
poor; for the holding or defending of private property; or for
any such thing. It is a design for a way of life in which there is
no wrongful self-interest needing to be curbed, and in which
all may accordingly be left in the hands of spontaneous love.
As Troeltsch says, 'The original Gospel ideal . . . lived on in
the idea of the Primitive State and of the absolute Law of Nature,
which kept ever before men's minds the ideals of freedom, of
union with God, of equality, and of love before God and in God.'[1]
And, as he goes on to say, this ideal was also kept before men's
minds, in however defective a form, by the life of the monastic
communities in their contrast to the life of even the most
Christianized general civilization. Yet the attempt to put this
ultimate Christian ideal into practice in the life of the world,
and even the attempt to put it perfectly into practice in the life
of a monastic community, would lead only to anarchy and chaos,
and to the disappearance even of that kind and degree of justice
which can be achieved through the adoption of the relative
ideal. It follows that the Christian's attitude to civilization
must be a double one. He must strive to bring it as near to
the Christian ideal of life in community as is possible in a world
of sinful men, but he must never give it his absolute approval
or unconditional loyalty; he must place in it only such a strictly
qualified hope as would, even if it were to suffer complete
shipwreck, leave his ultimate hope as securely anchored as
before.

[1] Op. cit., p. 175. Cf. also Sir Ernest Barker's account in the Introduction
to his translation of Gierke's *Natural Law and the Theory of Society*: 'The
absolute Law of Nature, in man's uncorrupted state of primitive grace, is a law
which knows no *dominium*. There is no *dominium* of government over subjects,
or of owners over property, or of masters over slaves: "by nature" men are free
from the State, they own all things in common, and they are equal to one another.
But there is also a relative Natural Law, adjusted to the change of man's nature
after the Fall, and relative to that change. The State, and property, and even
slavery, can all find their place in the scheme of this law; but they must all have
something of an ideal character, and rise above sin to the dignity of remedies
for sin, if they are to be really entitled to that place. The relative Law of Nature
is a sort of half-way house between an absolute ideal, vanished beyond recall,
and the mere actuality of positive law.' (p. xxxvii.)

No writer of our time has done more to clarify our minds concerning this double relation of Christianity to civilization than Dr. Niebuhr.

'The Christian conception of the relation of historical justice to the love of the Kingdom of God is', he tells us, 'a dialectical one. Love is both the fulfilment and the negation of all achievements of justice in history. Or expressed from the opposite standpoint, the achievements of justice in history may rise in indeterminate degrees to find their fulfilment in a more perfect love and brotherhood; but each new level of fulfilment also contains elements which stand in contradiction to perfect love.[1] . . . Laws and systems of justice . . . have a negative as well as a positive relation to mutual love and brotherhood. . . . This aspect of their character is derived from the sinful element in all social reality. They are merely approximations in so far as justice presupposes a tendency of various members of the community to take advantage of each other, or to be more concerned with their own weal than with that of others.[2] . . . No possible refinement of social forces and political harmonies can eliminate the potential contradiction to brotherhood which is implicit in the two political instruments of brotherhood—the organization of power and the balance of power.'[3]

At the same time Dr. Niebuhr has grasped the true 'dialectical' nature of the relation of justice to brotherly love much more completely than those theologians of the continental Confessional Movement who counsel a greater degree of Christian detachment from the values of civilization. Dr. Emil Brunner, for instance, well understands that justice is the presupposition of love, in the sense that 'a love which had not passed through the discipline of it must be capricious, unrealistic and sentimental'.[4] He likewise well understands that 'love must rise above justice'; and then he goes on to say that 'From the point of view of Christian faith no idea of perfect justice can possibly be conceived. For justice is *per se* imperfect. Only thinkers who do not know what love is can speak of justice as ultimate.'[5] Something important, however, seems here to be left out of account, namely, the use of justice as a necessary instrument of love's own self-expression. And this is what Dr. Niebuhr so effectively includes.

[1] *The Nature and Destiny of Man*, vol. ii, p. 255.   [2] Ibid., p. 261.
[3] Ibid., p. 268. Cf. also Dr. Niebuhr's Burge Lecture, *Do the State and Nation Belong to God or to the Devil?* (1937).
[4] *Das Gebot und die Ordnungen*, p. 437.   [5] Ibid., p. 436.

'This positive relation between rules of justice and the law of love must', he writes, 'be emphasized in opposition to sentimental versions of the love commandment according to which only the most personal, individual and direct expressions of social obligation are manifestations of Christian *agapē*. Both sectarian and Lutheran analyses of the relation of love to justice easily fall into the error of excluding justice from the domain of love. . . . Even if perfect love were presupposed, complex relations, involving more than two persons, require the calculation of rights.'[1]

The schema with which Dr. Brunner works seems to be that Christian love obtains only in strictly personal relationships, and justice only within the institutional orders of society; and that these latter are in no sense the creations of Christian love but are, even when ordained of God, to be organized in accordance with their own independent natural laws. Surely, however, these distinctions are much too rigidly drawn. Institutions and personal relations are much more necessary to one another than Dr. Brunner allows for. There is no institution that can flourish on the basis of legal compulsion alone, dispensing altogether with love; nor is there any personal relationship that is altogether independent of institutions, and into which there enters no element of justice. Even the love of husband and wife, or of mother and child, finds full expression only within the institution of the family, and without some admixture of impartial justice no family is properly ordered and governed. Obviously not even that least natural and most Christian of all institutions, namely, the Church, can be ordered on the basis of an *agapē* that refuses to express itself in terms of justice; but Dr. Brunner, while fully recognizing this, is able to do so only by drawing a further, equally clean-cut, and surely quite unacceptable, distinction between 'the Church of faith' which 'as such possesses no order'[2] and the Church as an institution. The true view of the relation of love to justice is that, while love goes far beyond justice, it uses justice as a necessary instrument of its own expression, congealing itself into the rigidity of law in proportion as relationships become too complex or too remote to be within the scope of direct personal knowledge and feeling.

It is accordingly wrong to think of earthly civilization and the Christian ideal of community as standing in simple anti-

---

[1] Op. cit., vol. ii, p. 260 f.   [2] Op. cit., p. 529.

thesis to one another; the true relation between them being rather of this 'dialectical' kind. The historical permeation of our society by Christian ideas and ideals is a development for which we must be profoundly thankful to the Lord of all history, and for the furtherance of which it is our duty to pray fervently, to work diligently, and to hope as bravely as we can. Yet we must never confuse this hope with that other which is the 'anchor of the soul, both sure and steadfast, and which entereth into that within the veil'.[1] For the earthly hope holds no promise even of its own imperfect fulfilment save as it refracts in the medium of the temporal the light of the hope that is eternal; so that the surest way to its disappointment would be that, in too much cherishing it, we should lose sight of that greater light which is its source. In proportion as a society relaxes its hold upon the eternal, it ensures the corruption of the temporal. All earthly civilizations are indeed corruptible and must one day perish, the *pax britannica* no less than the *pax romana*, and Christendom no less than Babylon and Troy. But if most have perished prematurely, it was largely as victims of their own proud illusions. And if our Western civilization is to prove more durable, it can only be in the strength of this more chastened estimate of its own majesty and this knowledge that 'here we have no continuing city'.

[1] Heb. vi. 19.